Collins

Social Studies for Jamaica Grade 7

Workbook

Series Editor: Farah Christian

William Collins' dream of knowledge for all began with the publication of his first book in 1819. A self-educated mill worker, he not only enriched millions of lives, but also founded a flourishing publishing house. Today, staying true to this spirit, Collins books are packed with inspiration, innovation and practical expertise. They place you at the centre of a world of possibility and give you exactly what you need to explore it.

Collins. Freedom to teach.

Published by Collins
An imprint of HarperCollins*Publishers*
The News Building, 1 London Bridge Street, London, SE1 9GF, UK

HarperCollins*Publishers*
Macken House, 39/40 Mayor Street Upper, Dublin 1, D01 C9W8, Ireland

Browse the complete Collins Caribbean catalogue at
www.collins.co.uk/caribbeanschools

10 9 8 7 6 5 4 3 2 1

ISBN 978-0-00-841399-6

British Library Cataloguing in Publication Data
A catalogue record for this publication is available from the British Library.

Publisher: Dr Elaine Higgleton
Commissioning editor: Kate Wigley
In-house senior editor: Craig Balfour
Author: Steve Eddy
Series editor: Farah Christian
Editorial project management: Oriel Square
Copyeditor: Andy Slater
Series designer: Kevin Robbins
Cover photo: Kwanza Henderson/Shutterstock
Typesetter: Jouve India Pvt. Ltd.
Production controller: Lyndsey Rogers
Printed and bound by: Martins the Printers
Maps: © CollinsBartholomew

Acknowledgements
The publishers gratefully acknowledge the permission granted to reproduce the copyright material in this book. Every effort has been made to trace copyright holders and to obtain their permission for the use of copyright material. The publishers will gladly receive any information enabling them to rectify any error or omission at the first opportunity.

MIX
Paper | Supporting responsible forestry
FSC™ C007454

This book contains FSC™ certified paper and other controlled sources to ensure responsible forest management.

For more information visit: www.harpercollins.co.uk/green

collins.co.uk/sustainability

Contents

Question Key

 Questions marked with a triangle test recall

Questions marked with a circle require some critical thinking and application of facts

Questions marked with a square require higher order thinking and analysis

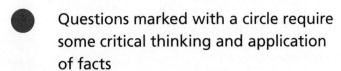

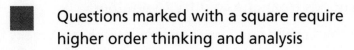 Questions marked with cogs are STEAM activities

1 Read pages 8–9 of the student book, 'What does it mean to be a Jamaican citizen?'.

a) Who is a citizen?

i) Someone who lives in a town or city

ii) Someone who belongs to a particular country

iii) Someone who lives in a city with a population under half a million

iv) Someone who receives an old age pension

b) What is the legal term describing someone living in a country who is not a citizen of it?

i) A partisan   ii) An international

iii) An alien   iv) An extraterrestrial

c) What is *not* a qualification for becoming a Jamaican citizen?

i) Being born in Jamaica

ii) Having Jamaican parents or grandparents

iii) Being a UK citizen and marrying a Jamaican

iv) Being able to sing the Jamaican national anthem

d) What is 'naturalisation'?

i) Becoming accepted as a citizen of another country

ii) Returning to nature

iii) Becoming a normal person

iv) Eating a healthy diet of non-processed foods

e) What is deportation?

i) Sailing out of a port (e.g. Kingston)

ii) The way someone stands and walks

iii) Being made to leave a country of which you are not a citizen

iv) Sending goods from one country to another

2 The law states that a child must be registered within six weeks of its birth. Who is responsible for registering a child born in:

a) a Jamaican hospital? _____

b) a Jamaican home? _____

3 Read pages 10–11 of the student book, 'What is the ideal Jamaican citizen?'. Put the statements made by a good Jamaican citizen on page 10 in order according to how important you personally think each one is. (1 = Most important.)

Statement	Importance
A. I love my country. I understand the history of Jamaica.	
B. I know the national anthem. I stand when it is playing.	
C. I obey the law.	
D. I vote in elections.	
E. I pick up litter.	
F. I know my rights and responsibilities.	
G. I respect the rights and freedoms of others.	

4 Explain your choices of the two most important and two least important statements.

_____

_____

_____

_____

5 Read pages 12–13 of the student book, 'Global citizen'. Put a 'J' for Jamaican or a 'G' for global next to each of these things a global or Jamaican citizen should do.

What you should do	J/G
Be patriotic	
Believe you can make a difference to the world	
Follow national laws	
Help reduce climate change	
Help to make the world fairer for everyone	
Learn the history, customs and traditions of your country	
Learn the skills to be able to work with people worldwide	
Protect the Jamaican environment	
Respect other cultures	
Respect the laws of other countries	
Respect the rights and freedoms of others	
Take part in community activities	

6 Read pages 14–15 of the student book, 'What is the Charter of Fundamental Rights and Freedoms?'. Match the rights or freedoms to the examples by adding the correct letter to the middle column.

Right or freedom		Example
a) The right to life		A. I can hold any religious beliefs I want, or none at all
b) The right to personal liberty		B. No one can kill me
c) Freedom of movement		C. No one can torture me
d) Freedom from inhuman treatment		D. No one can spy on me and my children at home
e) Enjoyment of property		E. No one can refuse to employ me because of my race or religion
f) Freedom of conscience		F. I can go wherever I want within Jamaica
g) Freedom of association		G. No one can take away anything I legally own
h) Respect for private and family life		H. I can meet up with whomever I choose
i) Freedom from discrimination		I. No one can enslave me, or imprison me unless I am convicted of a crime

7 Name three of these rights that prisoners would not have.

_____

_____

_____

8 Do you think prisoners should be allowed to vote? Explain your views.

_____

_____

_____

9 Research the work of Jamaicans for Justice. Make notes on one of their roles.

10 Read pages 16–17 of the student book, 'What are the rights of a child?'.

    a) What organisation introduced the idea of people having 'human rights'?

    _____

    b) What important declaration did the United Nations make in 1948?

    _____

    c) How many articles are there in the Universal Declaration of Human Rights?

    _____

    d) What set of human rights did the United Nations publish in 1990?

    _____

11 Write a paragraph about how children might be exploited by adults if it was legally permitted, and why this is morally wrong.

_____

_____

_____

_____

_____

_____

_____

12 One of the UN rights of children is: 'The right to express their opinions and have these listened to, and where appropriate, acted upon.' What does this mean for you in your daily life – for example at home or in school? Write a paragraph about your experience.

_____

_____

_____

_____

_____

_____

13 Read pages 18–19 of the student book, 'What happens when the rights of a child are not upheld?'. Then select *True* or *False* for each statement below.

a) Myanmar's government ensures that all Rohingya children receive an education. *True/False*

b) Some children have been tortured in Egyptian prisons. *True/False*

c) UNICEF is part of the United Nations. *True/False*

d) A UNICEF aim is for girls to be able to achieve as much as boys. *True/False*

e) UNICEF refuses to help children living in dangerous places. *True/False*

14 Why do you think a right to education is so important for children? Explain your ideas. You could consider:

- what you learn at school

- how going to school could change your life

- what you hope to achieve in your own education, and in adult life.

_____

_____

_____

_____

15 Read pages 20–1 of the student book, 'Which parts of the government are responsible for children's rights?'. Which government body deals with the following?

a) Fostering and adoption _____

b) Missing children _____

c) Child abuse _____

16 How did children's rights increase in 2014? Tick the correct answer.

a) They must now be given free bus passes.

b) They can now report violations of their rights themselves.

c) They were given the right to refuse education.

d) They now have a right to receive at least one birthday present every year.

17 **Write about how you think the rights of these three children are being violated.**

> Tyrone, aged 9, lives with his father, who is out every evening, and sometimes all night. He eats pizzas from the freezer and watches whatever online movies he chooses, including those depicting extreme violence. He finds it hard to sleep, and is always tired at school.

_____

_____

_____

_____

> Rita, aged 11, doesn't go to school because she is expected to work on her family farm and look after her younger brothers. Sometimes she works a ten-hour day. She doesn't get paid: her father says she has to earn her keep.

_____

_____

_____

_____

> Aston, aged 12, lives with his grandmother, who is too old to look after him properly. There is not much food in the house and he is usually hungry. Sometimes he steals food from a supermarket.

_____

_____

_____

_____

18 **On a separate sheet of paper, design an information brochure on children's rights. Think about:**

- who the brochure is aimed at
- key rights to include
- how the brochure could help children
- how to make it appealing.

19 **Read pages 22–3 of the student book, 'Individual and group civic responsibilities'. Tick which of these you regard as a civic responsibility.**

a) Working for a living if a job is available

b) Playing in a football team

c) Watching the same TV shows as your friends

d) Paying taxes if you work

e) Keeping Jamaica beautiful by not littering

f) Earning as much money as possible

g) Helping people in your community

h) Voting

i) Dressing smartly

20 **Look at the list above. Explain why you think one civic responsibility is important, and why something on the list above is *not* a civic responsibility.**

_____

_____

21 **Read pages 24–5 of the student book, 'How to take action'. Complete the paragraphs below using words from the word bank.**

Taking _____ is doing something to bring about _____ or political change. You could organise a _____, get publicity for a cause through the _____, take part in a _____, raise funds, or volunteer in your _____.

You could also become involved in an action group like Respect Jamaica, which _____ against discrimination, or Extinction Rebellion, which believes that we now have a _____ crisis, and that _____ must take more action to _____ the planet.

climate	action	save	petition	governments
community	campaigns	protest	social	media

22 Explain the words listed below, taken from case studies 2 and 3 on pages 24–5 of the student book. Use a dictionary (a book or online) if necessary.

Word	Meaning
emergency	
eliminate	
disruption	
compassionate	
advocacy	
abattoirs	
establishments	
amend	
constitute	
deterrent	

23 Which would you rather support, XR or the JSPCA? Do you feel that one of them does more important work than the other? Do you feel more sympathy for one than the other? Explain your thoughts.

_____

_____

_____

_____

_____

_____

_____

_____

_____

_____

_____

_____

_____

_____

1 Read pages 32–5 of the student book, 'What does it mean to be a national hero?'. Think of someone whom you personally regard as a hero. He or she could be dead or alive, famous or 'unsung'. Use the table below to explain in what ways they show at least three heroic qualities.

Name of hero:	
Quality	How shown
Courage	
Moral integrity	
Self-sacrifice	
Determination	
Honesty	
Ability to inspire	
Talent	

2 Explain what heroic qualities Mary Seacole showed (see page 33).

_____

_____

_____

3 How far do you think a leading sportsperson qualifies as a hero? Do you have a sporting hero? To be called 'heroic' does someone have to show more than talent? Write about your views. If you chose a sporting hero for activity 1, focus on a musician or artist here.

_____

_____

_____

4 Write a story in which someone does something heroic that shows courage and benefits others. Make notes below and write the story on a separate sheet.

_____

_____

_____

5 Read pages 36–9 of the student book, 'Who are Jamaica's national heroes and how did they contribute to Jamaica's development?'.

a) Even after slavery ended, the people of Jamaica continued to face many struggles. Paul Bogle, George William Gordon and Marcus Garvey fought against these. What did these three heroes fight against?

_____

b) What did Norman Manley and Sir Alexander Bustamante help to win for Jamaica? This event is recognised each year as a public holiday.

_____

6 Choose the correct answers.

a) Who led the 1831 Slave Rebellion?

i)   Nanny of the Maroons

ii) Samuel Sharpe

iii) Paul Bogle

iv) Marcus Garvey

b) What led to Paul Bogle being hanged?

i)   He insulted the Governor

ii) He refused to sing the national anthem

iii) He led a protest march on a courthouse

iv) He led a strike against working on Sundays

c) What did George William Gordon do with his land?

i)   Donated it to the people

ii) Grew an experimental strain of banana

iii) Let it go back to natural wilderness

iv) Divided it up and sold the sections cheaply to the poor

d) What political party did Marcus Garvey set up?

i)   People's Political Party

ii) People's National Party

iii) Jamaica Labour Party

iv) Communist Party of Jamaica

7 Nanny of the Maroons and Samuel Sharpe lived in different times but they had something in common. Visit the weblink on page 36 of the student book and, on a separate sheet, write one or more paragraphs explaining what they both fought against.

8 Sir Alexander Bustamante and Norman Washington Manley were cousins, and led opposing political parties. Write one or more paragraphs about:

- why you think both men have been made national heroes
- how it is possible in a democracy for leaders of opposing parties to both be heroes.

_____

_____

_____

_____

_____

_____

9 Examine the work of each of the national heroes, complete the table and tick the qualities displayed by each. Add more qualities of your own.

National Hero	Bravery	Determination	Self-sacrifice		
Nanny of the Maroons					
Samuel Sharpe					

 10 Research online to find out more about what life was like in Jamaica during the time each national hero lived. Produce a scrapbook (paper or digital). Include:

- three heroes from different periods
- pictures showing what life was like
- descriptions of conditions in each time period
- the dates of their lives
- explanations of how conditions made each hero behave as they did.

11 Read pages 40–3 of the student book, 'What are the awards and honours conferred upon Jamaicans?'. Complete the table below to show Jamaica's national honours and awards, their order of rank, what they are for, and examples of who has earned them.

Honour or award	Ranking	What for	Example
Order of the Nation		High political office	
	1		Nanny of the Maroons
Order of Merit			Bunny Wailer
	3	Given to foreign leaders	
Order of Distinction		Outstanding service	
	5		Amy Bailey

12 Select *True* or *False* for these statements about Jimmy Cliff.

a) He was awarded the Order of Merit. *True/False*

b) One of his best-known songs is called 'Many Rivers to Cross'. *True/False*

c) He plays one instrument – the guitar. *True/False*

d) He is famous for his calypso music. *True/False*

e) He contributed music to the film *Lion King*. *True/False*

13 Should national awards be given to musicians, artists or writers, who have not necessarily done anything brave or self-sacrificing? Explain your views.

_____

_____

_____

_____

_____

_____

2 National Heroes and Their Contributions to Jamaica's Development (cont.)

14 Read pages 44–7 of the student book, 'Who are some other outstanding Jamaicans?'.

a) In what area of achievement has Shelley-Ann Fraser Pryce excelled?

_____

b) Which Olympian athlete is Chairman of the Jamaica Bobsleigh and Skeleton

Federation? _____

c) What is the real name of the sportsperson whose nickname was 'Whispering

Death'? _____

d) Which Jamaican ranked at number four on the all-time list of 200 metres

runners? _____

e) What is Dr Thomas Lecky famous for? _____

f) What Jamaican achiever died aged 36 in 1981 and was given a state funeral?

_____

15 In your own words, summarise how Dr Thomas Lecky improved lives in Jamaica.

_____

_____

_____

16 Choose an outstanding Jamaican from pages 44–7, or another one you know about, and explain why you think they are particularly worthy of recognition.

_____

_____

_____

_____

_____

_____

_____

_____

17 Read pages 48–9 of the student book, 'How should we value the contribution made by these individuals?'.

a) Dr Thomas Lecky was a scientist. Name two other fields in which several Jamaicans have been recognised for their achievements.

_____

_____

b) What date was declared as Marcus Garvey Day in 2012? _____

c) About which Jamaican hero did Lee Scratch Perry write a song? _____

_____

d) Which hero is commemorated by a monument in Moore Town, Portland?

_____

18 Select *True* or *False* for these statements.

a) Paul Bogle's image appears on a Jamaican banknote. *True/False*

b) Bob Marley has had a mountain named after him: Mount Marley. *True/False*

c) Gerald Levy was a cricketing legend whose run-up to the wicket became known as 'the Bogle'. *True/False*

d) Nannyville Gardens in Kingston is named after Nanny of the Maroons. *True/False*

e) There is a road called Marcus Garvey Drive in Kingston. *True/False*

19 Imagine you have been asked to commemorate one of Jamaica's heroes. Choose a hero and write about what form of memorial you would choose, and why.

_____

_____

_____

20 Devise and carry out a survey among ten people.

a) For each person you question, find out how many national heroes your interviewee can both name and explain why they were nominated as heroes.

b) On a separate sheet of paper, present your findings in a bar chart that shows relative knowledge of each hero.

3   Jamaica's Cultural Heritage

 Read pages 56–9 of the student book, 'Culture and cultural background'.

a) What are customs, beliefs, arts and technology all part of?

_____

b) What are Pentecostalism, Rastafarianism and Islam all examples of?

_____

c) What is the key word that describes anything that we inherit from previous generations?

_____

2 Try this crossword to test your knowledge of the key concepts in this section.

Across	
6.	Customs, beliefs and arts are part of it
9.	Where we come from – our roots
10.	Acquired rather than inherited
11.	Someone from whom we are descended
12.	Constantly developing

Down	
1.	Made up of many cultures
2.	Type of pot used as an image of multiculturalism
3.	Country from which enslaved persons were taken
4.	Anything we inherit
5.	Traditional stories passed down generations
6.	Jamaican language
7.	Tribe who told Anansi stories
8.	Held in common with others

3 Fill in the gaps by adding words from the word bank.

We are not born with _____ cultural characteristics. Jamaican _____ do not automatically love reggae or _____ music. Culture is _____ and shared. It is also _____, meaning that it develops. There was no _____ until the 1960s.

Culture can be passed down over _____, like the Accompong Maroon Festival, or the Anansi _____ that originated in Africa. Culture also includes traditional _____, such as ackee and _____, and language. Jamaican _____ is an English-based creole language with _____ influences.

African	babies	calypso	dynamic	folktales	food
generations	inherited	learned	patois	reggae	saltfish

4 Look carefully at the 'Religions in Jamaica' pie chart on page 56 of the student book. Note that the population of Jamaica is about 3 million; a million is a thousand thousand (1 000 000). You can use a calculator.

a) How many Jamaicans are Protestant?

_____

b) How many Jamaicans have no particular religion?

_____

c) What religious group has about 30 000 members?

_____

5 Study the 'Ethnic origin in Jamaica' pie chart on page 57 of the student book.

a) How many Jamaicans have an ethnic origin other than black?

_____

b) What ethnic group in Jamaica has 180 000 members?

_____

c) For every person of East Indian ethnic origin, how many people are there of

black origin? _____

6 Read pages 60–1 of the student book, 'Jamaican national identity'.

a) What does the green of the Jamaican flag represent?

_____

b) A coat of arms is a convention dating back to medieval knights. What do the two figures on the Jamaican coat of arms represent?

_____

c) What does the motto on the coat of arms mean?

_____

d) What is the national bird of Jamaica?

_____

e) Why is the blue mahoe tree used for reforestation?

_____

f) Where did the ackee fruit originally come from?

_____

7 Write a paragraph about what you personally associate with Jamaican identity. Think about what images would immediately remind you of Jamaica if you saw them having been abroad for some time.

_____

_____

_____

_____

_____

_____

8 Read pages 62–3 of the student book, 'What are the material and non-material aspects of culture?'. On a separate sheet of paper and in your own words, explain the difference between material and non-material culture. Include at least one example of each not mentioned in this section.

9 See if you can divide these things into tangible and intangible. A *tangible* thing is touchable, or at least it can be felt by the senses. An *intangible* thing is more like an idea. Add 'T' or 'I' in each box.

a) The Blue Mountains ☐

b) The Rio Minho River ☐

c) Politeness ☐

d) Peas and rice ☐

e) Patois ☐

f) Bamboo craft ☐

g) Courage ☐

h) Anansi stories ☐

10 Remember, a proverb is an example of non-material culture. See if you can put these Jamaican proverbs into standard English and work out what they mean.

Proverb	Standard English	Meaning
a) Cack mowt kill cack		
b) Spit inna de sky, it fall inna yuh y'eye		
c) If you get your han' inna tiga mout, tek yu time and tek it out		
d) Ole fiyah tick easy fe ketch		
e) Yu shake man han, but yu noh shake im hawt		

11 Read pages 64–5 in the student book, 'Which are the ethnic groups in Jamaica?'.

a) Who were the first inhabitants of Jamaica?

i) the Spaniards

ii) Africans

iii) the Tainos

iv) Indians

b) Where did the Tainos come from originally?

i) Africa

ii) China

iii) Australia

iv) South America

c) The name from which 'Jamaica' stems is Xaymaca. What does it mean?

i) Land of gold

ii) Mountainous land

iii) Promised land

iv) Land of wood and water

12 Conduct research to find out more about the Tainos and answer the questions below.

a) What did the Tainos look like? _____

_____

b) What were some of the privileges of the cacique? _____

_____

c) What were some of the religious beliefs of the Tainos? _____

_____

13 The Tainos lived simple lives but they were considered creative. One reason for this is how they designed their homes to withstand hurricanes that sometimes hit the island.

Conduct research to find out about the Taino houses and make a model using recycled materials such as old newspaper or cardboard. Test your model to see how well it would stand up against the wind from a fan at home. Test it using the different fan speeds.

14 Read page 66, 'The Spanish settlers', and select *True* or *False* for each statement.

   a) Columbus discovered gold in Jamaica. *True/False*

   b) Columbus claimed Jamaica for Spain. *True/False*

   c) The first Spanish colony in Jamaica was called Sevilla la Nueva. *True/False*

   d) The Spanish regarded the Tainos as their equals. *True/False*

   e) The Spanish brought the first enslaved Africans to Jamaica in 1513. *True/False*

15 Read pages 66–7, 'The arrival of the British'. Complete the paragraph below using words from the word bank.

Penn and Venables attacked _____ in 1655 and _____ it from the Spanish, who _____. Before leaving, they _____ the enslaved Africans, who became the first _____. The British grew crops for _____ in England, especially sugar cane. Most of the _____ was done by enslaved _____.

Africans   freed   Jamaica   Maroons   sale   seized   surrendered   work

16 Read page 67 of the student book, 'Africans'.

   a) Why were enslaved Africans brought to the Caribbean?

   _____

   b) What parts of Africa were people taken from to work in the Caribbean?

   _____

   c) Tick which of these is not a tribe from which people were sold or kidnapped?

   i) Hausa   **ii)** Yoruba   **iii)** Igbo   **iv)** Zulu

   d) What did some Africans do on the ships to escape slavery?

   _____

   e) Why were enslaved Africans afraid to run away to the mountains?

   _____

17 Research why the British became interested in settling in the Caribbean and decided to challenge the Spanish for control. Explain on a separate sheet.

18 Find out how the enslaved Africans were acquired by the British and then taken to the Caribbean. Record your findings on a separate sheet.

19 The journey taken by enslaved people from Africa to the Caribbean was called the 'Middle Passage'. This was the second leg of the 'Triangular Trade'.

a) Where do you think the starting and finishing point of the triangle was?

  i) America　　　**ii)** Russia　　　**iii)** Britain　　　**iv)** France

b) Which of these was *not* one of the products taken from the starting country in the triangle for sale in Africa?

  i) Alcohol　　　**ii)** Cheese　　　**iii)** Cloth　　　**iv)** Weapons

c) What was the main product carried from the Caribbean to the finishing point of the triangle?

  i) Bauxite　　　**ii)** Bananas　　　**iii)** Sugar　　　**iv)** Flour

20 Look at the map on page 68.

a) To which area was the largest number of enslaved people taken?

_____

b) What were Songhai, Dahomey and Kongo?

_____

c) How many more enslaved Africans went to Brazil than went to North America?

_____

21 What was the main reason for Asians first coming to the Caribbean?

_____

_____

22 From what two countries did the first Jews come to the Caribbean?

_____

_____

23 Why did the Syrians and Lebanese first come to Jamaica?

_____

_____

24 Use the timeline on pages 68–9 to help you create a flowchart of Jamaican history in the boxes below. Summarise each event briefly in your own words and use arrows to show the development from one event to the next.

┌─────────────────────────┐   ┌─────────────────────────┐
│   │   │   │
│   │   │   │
│   │   │   │
│   │   │   │
│   │   │   │
└─────────────────────────┘   └─────────────────────────┘

┌─────────────────────────┐   ┌─────────────────────────┐
│   │   │   │
│   │   │   │
│   │   │   │
│   │   │   │
│   │   │   │
└─────────────────────────┘   └─────────────────────────┘

┌─────────────────────────┐   ┌─────────────────────────┐
│   │   │   │
│   │   │   │
│   │   │   │
│   │   │   │
│   │   │   │
└─────────────────────────┘   └─────────────────────────┘

┌─────────────────────────┐   ┌─────────────────────────┐
│   │   │   │
│   │   │   │
│   │   │   │
│   │   │   │
│   │   │   │
└─────────────────────────┘   └─────────────────────────┘

25 Imagine you are an enslaved African who decides to escape and join the Maroons in the Jamaican hills. On a separate sheet of paper, write an account of your escape up to the point where you meet the Maroons and know you have reached safety. You could include:

- your hopes and fears
- how you make your escape
- whether you escape alone or not
- what difficulties you faced.

26 Read pages 70–75 of the student book, 'How has each ethnic group contributed to Jamaica's culture and economy?'.

a) What are the Tainos' religious carvings called? _____

b) Who introduced most of the common domesticated animals to Jamaica?

_____

c) Which ethnic group is associated with ancestor worship? _____

d) Which group brought the Dragon Dance to Jamaica? _____

e) Which group introduced rice cultivation to Jamaica? _____

f) Which group banned Catholicism? _____

27 Imagine that members of each ethnic group are comparing their contributions to Jamaican culture. In each box, write the name of a group, what they might claim as their most important contribution, and why they have chosen it.

28 Imagine you work in a restaurant whose menu includes ingredients and dishes from each ethnic group. Think of a good name for the restaurant. Write a description to explain to customers what each dish is. Include its ethnic origins.

Restaurant name:	
MENU	
Bammy	
Escovitch Fish	
Pancakes	
Duckunno	
Mackerel Rundown	
Egg Plant Curry with Roti	
Sweet and Sour Pork with Pak Choy	

29 **Read pages 76–9, 'How have aspects of Jamaica's culture changed over time?'.**

a) How has the biblical quote 'They shall not make baldness upon their head' influenced a religion which developed in Jamaica in the 1930s?

_____

_____

b) Name one way in which Jamaican food has changed over the years.

_____

_____

c) i) What does the word 'reggae' come from?

_____

ii) What does this suggest about those who developed and enjoyed reggae?

_____

d) From what two musical styles did reggae evolve?

_____

e) How has technology influenced traditional children's games and storytelling?

_____

30 **Find out about the Bob Marley Museum on its website. You can also 'see' it digitally by going to Google Maps, searching for '56 Hope Rd, Kingston, Jamaica' and using Street View. (Drag the little person icon from the bottom-right corner to the address. Click and use your mouse pointer to pan around a view of the museum and house.)**

When you have done this, write two paragraphs on a separate sheet: one about why Bob Marley is important to Jamaica, and another one about what you would see on a tour at the museum.

31 **Conduct interviews with adults at home and in your community to find out ways in which they believe Jamaica's culture has changed. Write a two-paragraph report of your findings on a separate sheet.**

32 Read pages 80–2 of the student book, 'How are culture and cultural heritage preserved?'. Read the information on the Jamaica Conservation and Development Trust (JCDT) and the Jamaica National Heritage Trust (JNHT).

a) Which organisation is more concerned with the natural environment and Maroon culture? _____

b) Which organisation is more concerned with the 'built environment'?

_____

33 Now explore the websites of each organisation.

a) Explain what the JCDT considers to be so special about the communities of the Windward Maroons.

_____

_____

_____

b) Give brief details of three historic Jamaican buildings that are being protected by the JNHT.

_____

_____

_____

34 Read 'Our culture' on page 82. Write the introduction to a speech by a Member of Parliament arguing that government should give financial support to the JCDT and the JNHT because of the importance of preserving Jamaica's culture.

_____

_____

_____

_____

_____

_____

_____

_____

35 Read pages 84–7 of the student book, 'How effective are the institutions that currently help to preserve Jamaica's culture and heritage?'. Complete the table below using information from pages 84–5.

Festival	Commemorates	When
		January
Taino Day		
	Jamaican Independence	
		October

36 Look at the table of religious festivals on page 86 of the student book.

a) What festival is the 'festival of lights'? _____

b) Which festival is celebrated by two religions? _____

c) Which festival comes at the end of Ramadan? _____

d) What does Krishna Janmashtami celebrate? _____

e) Who brought Hosay to Jamaica? _____

37 Write a paragraph about a festival that you celebrate. Include what it celebrates, how you celebrate it, and how you feel about it.

_____

_____

_____

_____

_____

_____

_____

_____

38 Schools also play a role in preserving culture. Describe two ways in which schools help to preserve Jamaica's culture.

_____

_____

_____

_____

_____

_____

39 Look at page 87 of the student book.

a) Which of these is unlikely to be a historic site?

i) a fort   ii) a house   iii) a garage   iv) a battlefield

b) Which of these is a major cause of damage to historic buildings?

i) erosion   ii) weather   iii) birds   iv) frogs

c) Which of these is not a reason for delay in the restoration of buildings?

i) It is expensive   ii) It is time-consuming

iii) It requires expert knowledge   iv) It is a waste of time

d) Which of these is _not_ involved in the restoration of buildings?

i) The Jamaica Conservation and Development Trust

ii) Institute of Jamaica

iii) Jamaica Cultural Development Commission

iv) Jamaica National Heritage Trust

40 Do you believe that a building should be preserved because of its age? Does its history matter to you? If not, why does it matter to other people? Write a paragraph on your views.

_____

_____

_____

_____

_____

1 Read pages 96–9 of the student book, 'Physical resources and our environment'. Define these terms in your own words:

a) Resource

_____

b) Renewable

_____

c) Non-renewable

_____

2 Complete this crossword puzzle using the clues opposite. The answers are all key words from this section.

Across	
3.	Generated by sunlight
4.	Clear liquid essential to life
6.	Unprocessed
7.	Not replaceable
8.	Naturally occurring thing people can use
9.	Removal of trees
12.	Non-destructive use
13.	Taken out
15.	Substance plants grow in

Down	
1.	Electricity generated from running water
2.	Heat from underground
5.	Moving air
6.	Replaceable
10.	Liquid fossil fuel
11.	Invisible fuel
14.	Solid fossil fuel

3 **Complete this paragraph using words from the word bank.**

The sun is a natural _____. It provides heat and light, and enables plants to grow by _____. It can produce _____ through solar power. It _____ water from the sea, forming clouds, which produce _____. Water is essential to life. Plants cannot _____ without it. They also need soil to provide _____. In Jamaica, water also contributes to _____, in activities like rafting and kayaking.

electricity	evaporates	grow	nutrients
photosynthesis	rain	resource	tourism

4 **On a separate sheet of paper, draw a picture diagram showing the process of precipitation (the water cycle). Use arrows and colours to make the process clearer. Include:**

- the sun warming the sea so that water evaporates
- clouds forming
- rain falling onto the earth
- plants and trees growing, absorbing carbon dioxide, and releasing oxygen and moisture.

5. **Study the table on page 99 of the student book. Select *True* or *False* for each statement.**

   a) Burning oil as a fuel releases carbon dioxide and carbon monoxide into the air. *True/False*

   b) Trees 'breathe', absorbing oxygen. *True/False*

   c) When oil spills from tankers, it dissolves harmlessly in the saltwater. *True/False*

   d) Deforestation contributes to global warming. *True/False*

   e) Burning coal releases sulphur dioxide into the air. *True/False*

   f) Deforestation is good for wildlife as it creates new habitats. *True/False*

   g) There are limitless supplies of coal and oil in the world. *True/False*

   h) Trees can help to prevent flooding. *True/False*

6. **Write a paragraph on the environmental effects of burning fossil fuels – coal, oil and gas.**

   _____

   _____

   _____

   _____

   _____

   _____

   _____

   _____

7. **Research the use of these alternative, environmentally friendly energy sources:**

   - Solar
   - Hydro (water)
   - Wind
   - Geothermal

   Choose one source and write a paragraph about how it is used, or might be used, in Jamaica. Write about how it works, its benefits, and any disadvantages. Use a separate sheet of paper.

8 Read page 100 of the student book, 'The overuse of natural resources'.

a) Which fossil fuel has been used as a source of heat for centuries?

_____

b) Which fuel is used in modern homes for cooking, and is used to generate electricity?

_____

c) Which fuel is used to power planes and cars?

_____

9 Complete the paragraph below using words from the word bank.

Carbon _____ forms naturally in the atmosphere, but burning _____ fuels releases more of it. Carbon dioxide is the main _____ gas. Greenhouse gases trap the sun's heat, _____ the Earth and causing _____ change. This melts _____, raising sea _____. It also causes more _____ in the Caribbean.

climate	dioxide	fossil	glaciers
greenhouse	hurricanes	levels	warming

10 Look at the map on page 101 of the student book.

a) What mineral has Jamaica got that the USA hasn't got?

_____

b) What resource do Algeria, Libya and Saudi Arabia have?

_____

c) What mineral does Argentina have? _____

d) What do Rwanda, Myanmar and Vietnam all have in common?

_____

e) Which continent has the most diamond mines? _____

f) Which African country has oil and diamonds? _____

11 Read pages 102–5 of the student book, 'The importance of forests'. Then try the wordsearch using the clues. Words could appear vertically, horizontally or diagonally, in any direction.

```
N O I S S I M E T E O E E D
N B T A E I D G A O E D N S
X H S T G F E I T T I I I E
O E L M Y N F Y I S B O L I
R O U I O E O F B U O X L Z
A E D N N O R X A O S I Y Y
M O L E X X E E H N I D H T
A O S Y I O S E N E N E P A
Z G G B G H T R S G N N O O
O E N O L D A O S I A T E O
N L F I O N T S T D D T H A
S N Z E B N I I M N O N T A
E E D T A I O O O I I A G S
Y G M L L A N N G L N A T E
```

Clues

- You need it in air to breathe
- Form of carbon absorbed by trees
- Worldwide
- Given off by cars and factories
- Where animals and plants live
- These people often live in the forest
- Asthma drug
- Removal of trees
- Largest rainforest
- Wearing away by water or wind

12 On a separate sheet of paper, research one of the trees pictured on page 105. Make notes on:

- its appearance
- its habitat (where it grows, e.g. in rainforest)
- any special properties it has, e.g. being hard
- what it is used for.

13 On a separate sheet of paper, write a paragraph summarising why Jamaica should protect its trees. Consider:

- how they benefit the environment
- their uses
- how they contribute to the beauty of the landscape and our well-being
- how forests are threatened, e.g. by mining.

14 Read pages 106–7, 'Effects of misuse of the forest by humans'.

a) Which of these is *not* a cause of deforestation in Jamaica?

i) illegal logging   **ii)** agriculture   **iii)** mining   **iv)** beavers

b) Some of Jamaica's forest is *deciduous*. What happens to deciduous trees in winter?

i) They die   **ii)** They lose their leaves

iii) They hibernate   **iv)** They lose their branches

c) What happened to Jamaican forest between 2010 and 2014?

i) Much of it was blown down by hurricanes

ii) It halved in size due to logging

iii) It increased in size

iv) It became legally protected

15 Look at the list of ways in which you personally could help to reduce deforestation on page 107. On a separate sheet of paper, write one or more paragraphs about:

- which of these you do, or have done, already
- which you think you could quite easily do
- which you would be unlikely to do
- which you think would have the most benefit globally if everyone did it.

16 **Study the statistics, map and charts on page 106.**

a) What two changes in forestation are shown by the bar chart in 2013?

_____

_____

b) A hectare is 10 000 square metres – about the size of 2.5 football fields. By how many hectares did Jamaican forest increase between 2010 and 2014?

_____

c) Look at the pie chart. Calculate how many hectares of Jamaican forest are protected by law.

_____

d) What percentage of Jamaica is covered by unprotected forest, and which could therefore be cut down?

_____

17 **Read pages 108–13 of the student book, 'The natural resources of Jamaica'. Bauxite is the main mineral mined in Jamaica. Research to find out:**

- where it is found
- where it is mined
- what it is used for
- what problems are caused by bauxite mining.

Write one or more paragraphs on your findings.

_____

_____

_____

_____

_____

_____

_____

_____

_____

18 Land is an important resource in Jamaica, especially for farming. Look at the agriculture map on page 108.

a) Which crop is grown near the far north coast? _____

b) What is the main crop grown near the north-eastern coast?

_____

c) Which is grown more in Jamaica – coffee or sugar cane?

_____

19 Compare the agriculture map with physical and political maps of Jamaica in your atlases.

a) Name five rivers that would be important to sugar cane farmers.

_____

_____

_____

_____

_____

b) Name the crops that are grown on the plains of Jamaica.

_____

_____

_____

c) On a separate sheet, create a table showing the names of the different crops on the agriculture map and the parishes in which they are grown.

20 Look at the table on page 109 of the student book. Select *True* or *False* for each statement.

a) Some species of fish have declined a lot in Jamaican waters. *True/False*

b) The only reason for the decline in Jamaica fishing is pollution. *True/False*

c) As a bauxite producer, Jamaica is in competition with France and the Netherlands. *True/False*

d) Jamaica used to be the biggest producer of bauxite in the world. *True/False*

21 Read the case study on Ocho Rios on pages 110–11. Compare it with the version below which has eight factual mistakes. See if you can find and correct them.

> Modern-day Ocho Rios is a town of 30 000 people in Trelawny, but it started as a little mining village. It began to expand rapidly once tourism began there in the 1920s. Even by the 1970s the population had grown to 8 000. Its location high in the mountains made it ideal for tourism. More and more hotels were built, and people moved there from other parishes to retire. The town then grew in size, and restaurants, malls and entertainment centres were built – all solely to cater for the growing number of tourists.

Use separate sheets of paper for activities 22–25.

22 Imagine you are a town councillor in a large town that has rapidly expanded and has some or all of the problems listed on page 111. Think of a name for the town, and write the text of a speech to a town planning meeting saying what the problems are, their causes, and what you want to see done about them.

23 Read the case study on page 112 of the student book. Using details from the study, and adding some of your own, create a comic strip about the contamination as if it has just happened. Include:

- an attention-grabbing headline

- the basic facts, of what, where and who

- an account from a distressed local resident eyewitness

- a comment from a fisherman or an environmentalist

- a statement from the bauxite company.

24 Look at the pictures on page 112 and read the case study on page 113. Write a summary of what problems the residents of St Ann face.

25 Write about your own views on the pros and cons of bauxite mining in Jamaica.

26 Read pages 114–15, 'Economic policies and natural resources in Jamaica'. Then complete the paragraph below using words from the word bank.

An economic policy is a government _____ for how to develop the country's _____ by using national resources, creating _____ and earning national income. Sometimes a _____ has to try to _____ different policies. For example, mining _____ might create employment and earn income from big _____, but by spoiling the _____ it might interfere with the _____ of encouraging _____.

| balance | bauxite | companies | economy | employment |
| environment | government | plan | policy | tourism |

Use a separate sheet of paper for questions 27 to 29.

27 Create a document which lists at least four underused resources. Each must be linked to an income-earning industry. In each case, explain the earning potential and make recommendations of measures to ensure sustainability. For example, using bamboo for furniture.

28 Read the list of considerations for government on page 114 and imagine you are a government minister. Take three of these considerations and write the introduction to a speech suggesting your plans to deal with them. For example, you might make funding available to tackle a problem, propose a new law, or run an information campaign.

29 Imagine a greener, more environmentally friendly and sustainable Jamaica. Referring to 'Future resources that may be more sustainable' on page 115, write one or more paragraphs on how this could be achieved by your generation.

30 Design a system that would allow you to collect rainwater at home to conserve our water resources. Make a sketch of your system below and add notes to show what it looks like and how it works.

5 Utilising Our Resources: Human Resources

1 Read pages 122–3 of the student book, 'Different types of resources'. Referring to the first section on page 122, what three types of resource would be found in a bauxite factory?

_____

_____

_____

2 Complete the crossword using key concepts from pages 122–3.

Across	
1.	Learned abilities
3.	Saleable items
6.	Elderly people do it when they stop working
10.	Learning
12.	Work

Down	
2.	Earth seen as an asset for building or agriculture
4.	Tasks people perform for payment
5.	Relating to things you can see or touch
7.	To do with people
8.	Asset that can be used to make profit
9.	When two things need each other
11.	Number of people

3 Read pages 124–5 of the student book, 'Human resources and economic development'. Write a paragraph summarising the economic benefits of a well-educated population.

_____

_____

_____

_____

_____

_____

4 Think about your own education. What important things have you learned so far? What do you expect to learn in future? Will you go on to any further education after school?

a) Write a paragraph about how your education will enable you to play a part in Jamaica's economy.

_____

_____

_____

_____

_____

_____

_____

_____

b) Research and find out about a product that has been created by a Jamaican. Outline what knowledge and skills were required by the individual(s) in designing and creating the product. Use a separate sheet of paper.

5 Read pages 126–9 of the student book, 'The role of importing and exporting labour in Jamaica'. Divide the items in the table into things that Jamaica imports and things it exports, by writing 'I' or 'E' in the boxes.

Item	I/E
Bananas	
Mobile phones	
Sugar	
Computers	
Cars	
Aluminium	
Rum	

6 At various times, Jamaica has imported/exported labour from/to the countries shown below. Write 'I' for import and 'E' for export for each country. Give a reason for each one.

Country	I/E	Reason
United Kingdom		
China		
India		
Panama		
Cuba		

7 Read 'The Bank of Jamaica: We need more skilled workers' on page 127.

a) What is meant by 'Jamaica is beginning to approach its capacity limits in terms of skilled labour.'?

_____

_____

_____

b) What *two* options does the government have for increasing 'the pool of skilled workers'?

_____

_____

8 Read pages 128–9 of the student book. Imagine you are the head teacher of a secondary school. Write a speech to give to parents about what you understand to be the school's role and why it is important. You could consider:

- Transferable skills (skills that could be used in different situations, such as decision-making, or typing)
- Job opportunities in Jamaica or abroad
- Preparation for further education
- Teaching moral values
- Encouraging creativity and personal development.

_____

_____

_____

_____

_____

_____

_____

_____

_____

_____

9 Write what a parent might say about how much they agree with your speech.

_____

_____

_____

_____

_____

_____

_____

_____

_____

10 Read pages 130–1 of the student book, 'What is human resource development?'. Select *True* or *False* for each statement below.

a) HRD stands for Human Resource Development. *True/False*

b) After school, the only option for further education is university. *True/False*

c) People who have had further education often earn more money. *True/False*

d) Mentoring is carried out within employment. *True/False*

e) Succession training is training for several jobs, one after the other. *True/False*

f) The NVQ-J is only recognised in Jamaica. *True/False*

g) The JFLL says 13 percent of adult Jamaicans cannot read or write. *True/False*

11 Read pages 131–2 in the student book, 'What is earning a living?'. Explain these terms in your own words:

a) wage _____

b) salary _____

c) piece rate _____

d) perk _____

12 Read pages 134–5 of the student book, 'What are work ethics?'.

a) The adjective coming from 'ethics' (a noun) is 'ethical'. Write a sentence using this adjective that makes its meaning clear.

_____

_____

b) Explain the difference between doing something in the workplace that is illegal, and something that is unethical.

_____

_____

_____

_____

13 Dorcas is a secretary in an IT company. Her boss likes her because she is polite and always well dressed. However, she is bored with her job, so she often turns up late, especially if she knows that her supervisor won't be in the office that day. At other times she says the traffic was bad or her car wouldn't start. If she wants more time off, she says she had to see the doctor. Or she gets her boyfriend to phone and say she's sick.

Dorcas is getting married soon, so, in a quiet moment at work, she photocopied all the wedding invitations on the office copier. When her supervisor asked if she knew why so much copying paper was being used, Dorcas hinted that her colleague, Angelina, was stealing it. She's never liked Angelina because she complains when Dorcas doesn't do her share of the work.

Write a paragraph assessing Dorcas's work ethics. Include her good and bad points.

_____

_____

_____

_____

_____

_____

_____

_____

_____

_____

_____

_____

_____

_____

_____

14 Read pages 136–7 of the student book, 'What is a career?'. Select *True* or *False* for each statement below.

a) The only qualification you need in the world of work is determination. *True/False*

b) The life story and career of Usain Bolt could inspire many young Jamaicans, not just those who want to be athletes. *True/False*

c) Money is always more important than job satisfaction. *True/False*

d) Some people start successful careers by training for industries that are still developing. *True/False*

e) Some people are influenced in their career choices by the work their parents do. *True/False*

15 What are the advantages and disadvantages of being employed or self-employed? Use the table below to make notes on your ideas for different aspects of work. One example has been filled in for you.

Pros/Cons	Employed	Self-employed
Punctuality	Need to be on time each day.	
Job security		
Freedom to plan your own time use		
Wages/salary		
Colleagues		
Job satisfaction		
Opportunities for development		

16 Imagine that you leave school and are unemployed. You want to find a job in order to earn a living, enjoy a comfortable lifestyle, feel like a useful member of society, etc. You could just relax and enjoy the free time hanging out with friends, and wait for a job to turn up. List five things that you could do instead to help yourself develop a career.

a) _____

_____

_____

b) _____

_____

_____

c) _____

_____

_____

d) _____

_____

_____

e) _____

_____

_____

17 Read pages 138–9 of the student book, 'What types of industry are there?'.

a) How many main types of industry are there?

_____

b) If Level 1 is primary, what is the technical name for the 'Level 3' industries?

_____

c) Give an example of a job in the quaternary sector.

_____

18 Write the names of at least three jobs from the central 'job bank' in each named sector circle below (there are four listed for each sector).

Primary

Secondary

Aluminium smelting worker
Banana farmer
Banker
Bauxite miner
Builder
Clothing machinist
Distillery worker
Fisherman/woman
Forester
IT consultant
Journalist
Medical researcher
Nurse
Teacher
Waiter/waitress
Web designer

Tertiary

Quaternary

19 Read pages 140–1 of the student book, 'Jamaica's economic structure'. Write brief definitions of the following key terms.

a) Labour force

_____

b) Unskilled worker

_____

c) Permanent worker

_____

d) Temporary work

_____

e) Contract

_____

20 Answer these questions about the labour force in Jamaica.

a) Between what ages is someone considered to be part of the labour force?

_____

b) In what two categories from this section would you place the job of seasonal farm worker?

_____

c) Why would a contract be beneficial to both employer and worker?

_____

_____

21 Look at the pie chart on page 141.

a) Roughly what fraction of economic activity in Jamaica is in the services industries?

_____

b) If the population of Jamaica is 3 million, calculate the number of people working in manufacturing.

_____

22 Where do you see yourself finding work in future? Write a paragraph about what sort of work you expect to do.

_____

_____

_____

_____

_____

_____

_____

_____

_____

23 Read pages 142–3 of the student book, 'How do we classify careers? Groups 1–4'. Imagine you are a manager in a supermarket. Tick any tasks below which might be your responsibility.

a) Deciding what items to put on special offer

b) Ensuring that staff are trained in how to talk to customers

c) Making the tea or coffee at break times

d) Patrolling the aisles on the look-out for shoplifters

e) Ordering new uniforms for staff

f) Prioritising which shelves need to be topped up

g) Ensuring that different staff co-operate on related tasks

h) Boosting staff morale and awareness of objectives

i) Cleaning up customer breakages

j) Cleaning the staff toilets

24 Circle which of these workers is *not* classified as a professional.

accountant   security guard   architect   chemist   doctor   window cleaner

civil engineer   gardener   lawyer   logger   midwife   optician

waiter/waitress   scientist   taxi driver   teacher   town planner   vet

25 Read pages 144–5 of the student book, 'Career classifications: Groups 5–7'. Choose a job from Group 5 and explain how you would be suitable for the job and why you would like to do it.

_____

_____

_____

_____

26 Choose one job in Group 6 or 7 and explain why it is important to society. Use a separate sheet of paper.

_____

_____

_____

27 Research and make notes on one job from three different careers groups. Research could involve:

- looking in newspaper jobs sections or online for vacancies
- talking to a relative about their job
- finding information in a careers library.

_____

_____

_____

_____

_____

_____

_____

_____

28 Select one job from one industry and explain how any changes in employment by gender from 1960 to the present day has impacted that job.

_____

_____

_____

_____

_____

_____

_____

_____

29 Read pages 148–9 of the student book, 'How have jobs and careers evolved over time in Jamaica?'. Research and make notes on how new technologies, such as computing and the internet, and the problems of climate change, are creating new job markets. Use a separate sheet of paper.

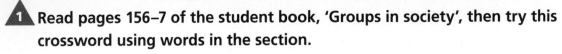

1 Read pages 156–7 of the student book, 'Groups in society', then try this crossword using words in the section.

Across	
2.	Your relatives
5.	Sense that we are part of a group
6.	Your class here is a secondary group
8.	Several people sharing a common purpose
10.	This group shares a faith
11.	Structured, with rules
12.	Relate to others; e.g. in a school class
13.	Your class at school is this type

Down	
1.	Relating to society
3.	Casual, like a sports club
4.	Like a football crowd, not lasting
6.	This club is an informal group
7.	A family is this type of group
9.	Oneness

2 **Read pages 158–9 of the student book, 'The functions of groups'.**

a) In your own words, explain the word 'function'. You could use an example, such as the function of a washing machine.

_____

b) Look at the diagram on page 158. In your own words, explain 'self-esteem'.

_____

c) In your own words, explain 'companionship'.

_____

3 **Referring to the diagram and the speech bubbles on pages 158–9, choose three of the functions and explain how being in a group has provided you with one of the benefits listed in the diagram. If you wish, it could be a different group for each one.**

a) Function _____

_____

_____

b) Function _____

_____

_____

c) Function _____

_____

_____

4 **Suggest some possible functions and activities of these groups:**

a) A fishing club

_____

_____

b) A book group

_____

_____

c) A food cooperative

_____

_____

d) An environmental group

_____

_____

5 Read pages 160–1, 'The characteristics of groups'. Then try the wordsearch.

There are 12 words which could appear vertically, horizontally or diagonally, and in any direction. They include the key vocabulary on page 161, and five words from the diagram on page 160. a) to e) are clues to the extra words.

```
S  O  E  B  D  X  X  K  G  H  I  W  S  M  J
U  A  F  D  A  X  F  X  I  N  C  I  T  O  C
F  G  N  U  I  R  M  E  Y  P  H  W  R  V  O
R  F  M  C  R  D  R  R  I  F  H  Q  U  W  O
C  M  H  F  T  A  A  H  S  V  Q  E  C  M  P
R  I  N  V  R  I  S  Y  M  B  O  L  T  S  E
U  B  G  C  U  R  O  I  D  K  P  Q  U  A  R
U  Q  H  C  E  F  D  N  T  G  P  R  R  W  A
F  Y  A  B  Z  E  H  F  S  O  L  K  E  Y  T
C  V  M  W  N  O  I  T  C  A  R  E  T  N  I
W  E  L  T  B  Y  T  I  R  O  H  T  U  A  O
M  C  I  J  S  S  Y  B  W  X  H  S  G  K  N
F  T  V  I  W  B  B  R  H  F  W  M  M  V  H
Y  C  W  H  P  U  R  P  O  S  E  Y  R  P  M
U  E  W  W  U  N  L  D  L  R  M  E  G  Y  A
```

a) Working harmoniously with others

b) A sense of who you are

c) Aim or goal

d) Relating, e.g. in conversation

e) Being in a group (for formal groups there could be a fee)

6 'All groups need structure and leadership.' How far do you think this is true? Write a paragraph on your views. Refer to at least one group of which you have been a member.

_____

_____

_____

_____

_____

_____

_____

_____

_____

7 You are interested in forming a group in your community. On a separate sheet of paper, outline the ideas you have for this group. Consider the following:

- The purpose of forming the group and the functions the group will carry out.

- How individuals may become members of the group and who will be targeted to become members.

- Symbols that will be used by the group.

- Some activities that the group will be engaged in to help members bond and the group to carry out its functions.

8 Read pages 162–3 of the student book, 'Institutions and types of social institutions'. Name the five basic institutions that serve the needs of society.

a) _____   b) _____

c) _____   d) _____

e) _____

9 What are norms? Explain and give two examples from different institutions.

_____

_____

10 A sentence on page 162 says: 'Socialisation is the process of internalising norms and values of a society.' Explain this, using your own words as much as possible.

_____

_____

_____

_____

11 Read pages 164–5 of the student book, 'Agents of socialisation'.

a) What are the two types of socialisation?

_____

b) Give an example of how you have been influenced by:

i) informal socialisation

_____

ii) formal socialisation

_____

12 **Read pages 166–7 of the student book, 'Understanding social norms'.**

a) Name one social norm that you would observe at a family dinner.

_____

b) Name a social norm that you would observe in a busy shop that only has one till.

_____

c) How would you behave if you passed someone on a path:

i) in a forest

_____

ii) on a busy city street?

_____

13 **Suggest the reason(s) for the difference in your answers to i) and ii) above.**

_____

_____

14 **Look up and make notes on:**

a) where the word *taboo* comes from

_____

_____

_____

b) examples of religious taboos.

_____

_____

_____

15 **Have you noticed that different age groups follow different social norms? For example, there might be a difference in the way that you would greet a friend, and how your grandparents would do the same thing.**

Write a paragraph about these differences, and how you think social norms in Jamaica might be changing over time. Use a separate sheet of paper.

16 Read pages 168–9 of the student book, 'Different types of groups'. Write one or more paragraphs about how your membership of primary and secondary groups, and formal and informal groups, has changed over the years since you were a young child.

_____

_____

_____

_____

_____

_____

_____

_____

17 Read pages 170–1, 'Differences between groups'. Select _True_ or _False_ for each statement.

a) Primary groups are small. _True/False_

b) A trade union is an example of a primary group. _True/False_

c) Secondary groups may have formal rules. _True/False_

d) Membership of secondary groups is temporary and voluntary. _True/False_

e) Formal groups usually have spontaneous activities. _True/False_

f) Formal groups have defined roles. _True/False_

g) Children playing on the street form a formal group. _True/False_

18 How would you classify the group of teachers at your school? Do they fall into the category of a primary or secondary group, formal or informal group? Explain your classification of them.

_____

_____

_____

19 Think of a primary informal group you are in. On a separate sheet of paper, write about what unwritten or even unspoken rules it has. (Consider what behaviour would get you into trouble in this group.)

20 Read pages 172–3 in the student book, 'Benefits of groups'. Complete the sentences using words from the word bank.

a) Groups can give a sense of belonging, which makes an individual feel more _____.

b) Members of a group that tackle a _____ can feel a sense of solidarity.

c) An important part of group membership is _____ – commitment to supporting fellow members.

d) Groups can choose a course of _____ together – make decisions.

e) Group members can _____ each other new skills.

problem   action   teach   secure   loyalty

21 Choose three of the statements above. Give an example of a situation in which each might work in a particular group.

_____

_____

_____

22 Read about group cohesion on page 173 of the student book. Write a story in which a group overcomes an obstacle to its cohesion because it has at least three of the strengths listed there. Continue on a separate sheet if necessary.

_____

_____

_____

_____

_____

_____

_____

_____

_____

23 Read pages 174–5 of the student book, 'Overcoming group issues'. Which of the factors listed on page 174 is shown in each case below?

a) 'How are we ever going to get anywhere if you miss band practice because you say you have to "take care of business"?'

_____

b) 'I thought you said to meet at the café. I waited there half an hour.'

_____

c) 'Half of us want to sing gospel, the other half are into JaFolk Mix!'

_____

24 In your own words, explain how each of these concepts might work in a group, including an example of each:

a) Compromise

_____

_____

b) Peer pressure

_____

_____

c) Cooperation

_____

_____

25 There are different ways to decide things in a group. For example:

- A leader decides everything, e.g. what songs a choir sings.
- The group votes on every issue.
- A leader presents two or three options and calls a vote.
- Decisions are made by an elected committee.

Explain which option you prefer, and why.

_____

_____

_____

_____

26 Read pages 176–9 in the student book, 'Leadership' and 'The role of a leader'. Make a list of at least four leaders, either officially (like a head teacher), or unofficially (like the leader of a social group). Say briefly why each one is a leader.

_____

_____

_____

_____

_____

_____

27 Read the definitions of authority types on page 177 of the student book. Which definition do you think applies to the leaders spoken about in these bubbles?

A. 'And it has been declared that the new leader of the Jamaica First Party is …'

B. 'Her Majesty has issued a royal decree requiring that from henceforth …'

C. 'I don't know what it is – there's just something about him that makes people believe in him.'

A. _____

B. _____

C. _____

28 Research one of these leaders, Portia Simpson-Miller; Toussaint Louverture; Haile Selassie, Emperor of Ethiopia; Benazir Bhutto and write at least two paragraphs about them on a separate sheet. Include:

- their nationality
- when they were born and died (if no longer alive)
- what gave them their authority
- what their main achievements were.

1 Read pages 186–9 of the student book.

a) Write your own definition of what a 'family' is.

_____

b) Rearrange the jumbled descriptions and identify each type of family.

Sentence	Type
a) her children or with one parent living his	
b) a family or one in which both children have parents from previous relationships	
c) a household in which younger siblings are absent so the older brothers and sisters take care of the parents	
d) such as grandparents or larger siblings family with a family members married additional	
e) a children living their together one in household mother father and with	

2 In your own words, explain the meaning of 'union'.

_____

_____

3 For each type of family below, state one possible advantage and one disadvantage from the list on page 188 of the student book. Use a separate sheet of paper.

Nuclear   Extended   Reconstituted   Sibling household   Single parent

4 Read pages 190–1 of the student book, 'Family history'.

a) Select *True* or *False* for each statement.

  i)   Your ancestry is where you were born. *True/False*

  ii) Customs are behaviours which are repeated, often regularly. *True/False*

  iii) A family tree is a geological diagram. *True/False*

  iv) A patriarchal family tree shows the lineage on the father's side. *True/False*

  v)   A family tree showing both sides of the family is bilingual. *True/False*

  vi) A matriarchal family tree shows the lineage on the mother's side. *True/False*

b) On a separate sheet of paper, draw your own family tree showing at least three generations.

5 Read page 192 of the student book, 'Functions of the family'.

a) What word refers to both brothers and sisters? _____

b) Wesley's father has a sister, Jessica. What relation is Jessica to Wesley?

_____

c) Jessica has a son, Aidan. What relation is Aidan to Wesley? _____

d) If Wesley has siblings, and they have daughters, what relation are they to him?

_____

e) If you share a set of grandparents with someone, and this person is not your sibling, what relation are they to you? _____

6 Select an article from the newspaper or another appropriate source and consider whether the incident described is a result of family cohesion, or the lack of. Be sure to include at least three references in your answer to support your position.

_____

_____

_____

_____

7 Based on the source you used, explain how family conhesion could have prevented what happened.

_____

_____

_____

_____

8 The speech bubbles below contain something that a family member might say. Who do you think each person is? What do you think of their attitude?

A. Look – I've been down the mine since 8.00am. You've got a soft job at the bank. Why can't you put a meal on the table _and_ get the kids ready for bed?

_____

_____

B. It's not fair! Why do you always get to boss the rest of us around just because you're the oldest?

_____

_____

C. Listen, Leroy. Your dad's not around anymore, so you're going to have to help around the house whether you like it or not. I can't do everything.

_____

_____

D. Don't worry. I can look after the kids when they get home from school till you come home. I want to help out, and it makes me feel I'm still good for something!

_____

_____

9 Read pages 193–5 of the student book, 'The five functions of the family'. Which family function is suggested by each speech bubble?

A. We all miss him, but we still have each other, and we'll get through this together.

B. OK, here's the deal. You wash the car each week and I'll raise your pocket money to $3. That will give me a bit more time to work to support this family!

A. _____

B. _____

10 Read pages 196–9 in the student book, 'My roles and responsibilities'. What do you understand by these phrases?

a) Gender pay gap

_____

b) Female equality

_____

c) Role model

_____

d) Traditional family roles

_____

_____

11 Study the table on page 199 carefully. Then write one or more paragraphs about how family roles are changing in Jamaica and what your views are on this. You could write about:

- traditional roles
- why roles are changing
- whether women should get paid the same as men for the same work
- what you think would be best for Jamaican society and why.

_____

_____

_____

_____

_____

_____

_____

_____

_____

12 Read pages 200–2 in the student book, 'What are some of the challenges faced in Jamaica?'. Select *True* or *False* for each statement.

a) One in four children in Jamaica lives in poverty. *True/False*

b) Poor parenting skills can lead to teenagers joining gangs. *True/False*

c) The National Family Planning Board helps families to make plans. *True/False*

d) The Child Development Agency is responsible for care and protection of children. *True/False*

e) The National Health Fund helps people to pay for recreational drugs. *True/False*

f) UNICEF Jamaica's current priorities include lifelong learning. *True/False*

g) The Maxfield Park Children's Home was established in July 1981. *True/False*

13 Complete the paragraph below using words from the word bank.

A number of _____ agencies exist to _____ families. These deal with areas such as family _____ and sexual _____, foster _____ placement, child poverty and paying for _____ drugs for people with long-term _____. UNICEF is an NGO (non-governmental organisation) that helps _____.

care	children	government	health
illnesses	planning	prescription	support

Use separate sheets of paper for activities 14 and 15.

14 Write a paragraph about what you see as the main problems facing Jamaican families and what would be needed to solve them, or at least reduce their impact.

15 Design an information flyer to distribute in your community to tell families about the different agencies that could help them to overcome some of the challenges they face. Describe the layout for the flyer and outline the information that will be placed on it.

8　Movements of the Earth

1 ▲ Read pages 212–25 of the student book, 'The effects of movements of the Earth'.

a) What word describes the Earth's spinning on its axis? _____

b) What word describes the Earth's circling of the Sun? _____

2 Choose the correct answer for each question.

a) What is the solar system?

   i)   A home-heating method using solar energy

   ii) The Sun and the planets and other objects going round it

   iii) The system through which the Sun heats the Earth

   iv) A radio system used by submarines

b) In which direction does the Earth spin?

   i) East to west   **ii)** North to south

   iii) South to north   **iv)** West to east

c) What keeps the planets and other objects in orbit round the Sun?

   i) Gravity   **ii)** Electro-magnetism

   iii) Rotation   **iv)** The Moon

d) What is the Earth's axis?

   i)   Its reason for existence

   ii) An imaginary line running north–south through its centre

   iii) An imaginary line running west–east through its centre

   iv) Its distance from the Sun

e) What is the summer solstice?

   i)   The shortest day of the year

   ii) The first day of spring

   iii) The longest day of the year

   iv) The first day of autumn

3 Add the names of the planets (and the Moon) in their correct order of distance from the Sun. Try it from memory, then check on page 212 of the student book.

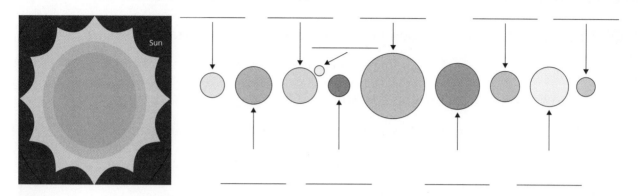

4 Fill in the gaps using words from the word bank.

Day and night are caused by the Earth turning on its _____ every day so that at any moment one half of the planet is _____ the Sun and the other half is facing away from it.

The Earth is _____ at 23½ degrees on its axis, so that the _____ hemisphere is tilted towards the Sun during _____, while the southern _____ is tilted away from the Sun at that time. This means that when it is summer north of the _____, it is winter _____ of it.

Jamaica is fairly close to the equator – the _____ between the north and south poles, so it does not have extreme _____.

equator	facing	hemisphere	midpoint	northern
seasons	south	tilted	axis	summer

5 Use foam balls or create balls using old newspaper to make models of the Earth and Sun to illustrate rotation and its effects on the Earth. Show the tilt of the Earth on its axis and think about the size of the Earth compared with the Sun.

8 Movements of the Earth (cont.)

6 Tick the features that helped to make life possible on Earth.

a) The Earth is part of a fairly stable solar system.

b) The Earth revolves around the Sun in 365.25 days.

c) The Earth is at an ideal distance from the Sun for using its energy.

d) The ozone layer blocks harmful rays from the Sun.

e) Heat within the Earth creates volcanoes.

f) Our moon helps to maintain the Earth's tilted angle, stabilising its seasons.

g) Without the shade provided by Venus and Mercury, Earth would overheat.

h) Lunar ocean tides helped early life to migrate from the sea onto land.

i) Earth has a plentiful supply of water.

7 Using some of the information in your answers to the previous question, write one or more paragraphs about how likely you think it is that life could be found elsewhere in the universe.

_____

_____

_____

_____

_____

_____

_____

_____

_____

_____

_____

_____

8 Research conditions on Mars. Write one or more paragraphs describing what difficulties human beings would have to overcome in order to live there. Use a separate sheet of paper.

9 Read pages 216–17 of the student book, 'World geography: locating places'. Which way do lines of latitude go round the Earth? Tick the correct answer.

- Horizontally (east–west)
- Vertically (north–south)

10 Add the labels in the box to the lines of latitude shown on the graphic. Also mark the North Pole and the South Pole.

| Equator | Tropic of Cancer | Tropic of Capricorn |
| Arctic Circle | | Antarctic Circle |

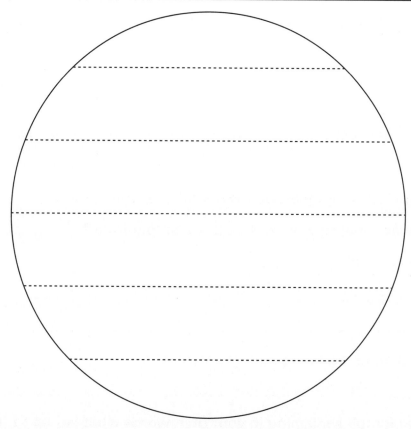

11 Explain:

a) what the Prime Meridian is

_____

_____

b) how it relates to the International Date Line

_____

c) what happens if you cross the Date Line.

_____

12 Read pages 218–19 in the student book, 'History of longitude and latitude'. Select *True* or *False* for the following statements.

a) The Phoenicians lived in the Middle East. *True/False*

b) Greek astronomer Hippocrates originated the use of gridlines for latitude and longitude. *True/False*

c) The word 'circumference' means the distance all the way round something round. *True/False*

d) Knowing the circumference of the Earth helped the ancient Greeks to draw maps. *True/False*

e) The ancient Greeks calculated latitude by the use of archaeology. *True/False*

f) Columbus was trying to find Africa when he found Jamaica. *True/False*

13 Answer the following questions about latitude and longitude.

a) Which was easier to work out, latitude or longitude? _____

b) What was 'dead reckoning'?

_____

_____

c) Why was dead reckoning not very accurate?

_____

14 Write a paragraph explaining in your own words what led up to John Harrison's invention of a device that could measure longitude at sea.

_____

_____

_____

_____

_____

_____

_____

15 Read pages 220–1 in the student book, 'Locating the Caribbean'. What would you find:

a) 100 miles west of Haiti? _____

b) 90 miles north of Jamaica? _____

c) 390 miles south-west of Jamaica? _____

16 Which country is located at each of the following points?

a) 15 degrees North, 90 degrees West _____

b) 5 degrees North, 55 degrees West _____

c) 20 degrees North, 75 degrees West _____

d) 10 degrees North, 85 degrees West _____

17 Look at the map on page 221. In which counties are these Jamaican parishes?

a) Trelawny _____ **b)** St Mary _____ **c)** Portland _____

18 Read pages 222–3 in the student book, 'Time zones'. At noon GMT, what time is it in:

a) New Orleans _____ **b)** Miami and Jamaica _____ **c)** Berlin _____

19 At 3:00 pm GMT what time is it in:

a) Anchorage, Alaska _____ **b)** Moscow _____ **c)** Tokyo _____

20 On these clocks, write the name of any city where it is the given time when it is noon in London (GMT). The first one has been done for you. Note that it is a 12-hour clock, so you could write the name of a city that is ahead of London, or behind. So, instead of Kingston (7 a.m. five hours behind), it could say 'Krasnoyarsk (7 p.m. seven hours ahead).

Kingston   **a)** _____   **b)** _____   **c)** _____

21 Read pages 224–5 of the student book, 'Time, climate, seasons and human activities'.

a) What is the term for how a year is divided into different weather in a particular place?

_____

b) What are climate zones?

_____

_____

22 Look at the map on page 224. In what climate zones are the following places:

a) United Kingdom _____ b) Jamaica _____

c) Central Australia _____ d) India _____

e) Iceland _____

23 Name a country where:

a) temperatures can be as high as 50 °C but can be much lower at night

_____

b) there is only one season throughout the year

_____

c) there is rainfall all year round, but especially in autumn and winter

_____

d) winter temperatures can drop to −50 °C

_____

e) there is about 1500 mm of rain per year.

_____

f) Choose one country and explain how technology made life better for its citizens.

_____

_____

24 Read pages 226–7, 'How the climate affects how we live'. Select *True* or *False* for the following statements.

a) Cricket in the Caribbean is played November–May. *True/False*

b) People usually wear shorts and T-shirts in northern Russia. *True/False*

c) Malaria is spread by mosquitoes in tropical areas. *True/False*

d) The mountains of New Zealand and the USA are popular for skiing. *True/False*

e) Ethiopia has the ideal climate for crop-growing. *True/False*

f) It is hard to grow crops in Alaska. *True/False*

25 Write a paragraph about how the climate affects your life in Jamaica.

_____

_____

_____

_____

_____

_____

26 Choose a country whose climate you think would be very different from that of Jamaica. Research and make notes on:

- the seasons, rainfall and temperatures
- what sort of agriculture, if any, goes on there
- what animals you might find there
- how people's lives there are affected by climate.

_____

_____

_____

_____

_____

_____

_____

_____

_____

1 Read pages 234–5 of the student book, 'Relationships between communities'. Name the three different types of integration.

_____

_____

_____

2 Try this crossword that uses key words from this section.

Across	
5.	Relating to an area, e.g. the Caribbean
7.	Helping each other; being able to depend on each other
10.	Working together, becoming part of something

Down	
1.	To rely on or be controlled by something
2.	Involving two countries, e.g. an agreement
3.	Working together and helping each other
4.	An exchanged promise
6.	Type of integration when culturally diverse people develop mutual respect
8.	Relating to a shared genetic make-up
9.	Relating to trade and productivity

3 Referring to page 235, write a paragraph explaining why, in the 1950s, Caribbean countries began to consider integrating with each other. Explain how they started and how it continues today.

_____

_____

_____

_____

_____

_____

4 Read pages 237–8, 'Community development and cooperation'. Explain the difference between these two concepts. State an example for each.

_____

_____

_____

_____

5 Summarise what the Linstead Community Development Committee does.

_____

_____

_____

_____

6 Explain what you understand by 'alternative dispute resolution methodologies', as used by the Peace Management Initiative. Look up in a dictionary any of the words you're not sure you understand.

_____

_____

_____

7 Design a poster for the T3M recording studio that will appeal to the kind of young people they aim to reach. On a separate sheet of paper, either roughly sketch and make design notes, or produce an actual poster.

8 Read pages 238–9 of the student book, 'Regional cooperation: The West Indian Federation'. Explain what the West Indian Federation was and its main aim.

_____

_____

_____

9 Complete this paragraph about the Federation being disbanded, using words from the word bank.

Trinidad and Tobago and _____ were no longer prepared to _____ most of the Federation's _____. Smaller countries did not want more _____ countries to _____. There was disagreement about where to have the _____ of the Federation. Jamaica felt that the Federation was holding back its _____ from Britain. Leaders preferred to lead their own _____ rather than the Federation. Jamaica held a _____ in 1961 and voted to _____.

capital	costs	dominate	independence	countries
Jamaica	leave	powerful	referendum	bear

10 Read pages 240–1, 'Regional cooperation: CARIFTA'. List countries that joined CARIFTA that were not in the West Indian Federation.

_____   _____   _____

11 Tick the things CARIFTA encouraged member states to do:

a) buy and sell more goods between themselves

b) close the gender pay gap in the region

c) diversify and expand the variety of goods and services available in the region

d) ensure cooperation on environmental issues

e) make sure there was fair competition, especially for smaller businesses

f) make sure that the benefits of free trade were shared fairly among member states

g) allow free movement of workers within member states

h) develop a shared defence policy

12 Write the introduction to a speech that a government minister might have made to ministers of other Caribbean countries to persuade them to sign on to CARIFTA.

_____

_____

_____

_____

_____

_____

13 Read pages 242–3 of the student book, 'Regional cooperation: CARICOM and CSME'. Which of these is not an objective of the CSME?

a) Improved standards of living

b) Full employment

c) Redistribution of wealth within member states

d) Coordinated economic development

e) Expansion of trade and economic relations with other states

f) Free dentistry for citizens of all member states

g) Free movement of money and skilled labour between member states

h) The right to set up a business in another member state

i) A ban on bauxite mining

j) Freedom from taxes on goods passing between member states

14 List the member states of CARICOM. Then, explain why the transition was made from CARIFTA to CARICOM.

_____

_____

_____

_____

_____

_____

_____

15 Which Caribbean country is not in CARICOM because it is part of the USA?

_____

16 Suggest a likely reason for Cuba not being part of CARICOM.

_____

17 Read pages 244–5 of the student book, 'Cooperation in the Caribbean: Sport'.

a) Why were the CARIFTA games set up?

_____

b) In what year were the CARIFTA games first held?

_____

c) What are the age categories for the games?

_____

18 What do the careers of Usain Bolt, Veronica Campbell-Brown and Kim Collins all have in common?

_____

19 Write a dramatic description of *either* an event in the CARIFTA games *or* a cricket match between the West Indies and another country.

You could write your description from the viewpoint of:

• a competitor or player (use first person – 'I …')
• a sports commentator (use present tense – 'And Bolt is edging up on the inside …')
• someone in the crowd.

_____

_____

_____

_____

_____

_____

_____

20 Read pages 246–7, 'Cooperation in the Caribbean: Education and medicine'.

a) What does UWI stand for?

_____

b) When did UWI become independent?

_____

c) Where are UWI's three main campuses?

_____

_____

_____

21 Tick which of these the Caribbean Environmental Health Institute (CEHI) advises on:

a) water supplies

b) sewage treatment

c) teenage TV viewing

d) solid waste management

e) water resources management

f) beach pollution

g) sports events

h) air pollution

i) disaster preparedness

j) crime prevention

k) natural resources conservation

l) agricultural productivity

22 Think of a university degree course that you think you might like to do at UWI. Research the course and make notes on it. Then write what you might say in an interview to answer the question, 'What do you hope to get out of this course?'

_____

_____

_____

_____

_____

_____

_____

_____

_____

23 Read pages 248–9 of the student book, 'Cooperation in the Caribbean: Culture and disaster preparedness'. Sort these jumbled phrases into aims of CARIFESTA.

a) to people the region the life depict of the of

_____

b) to flourish a climate in which create art can

_____

c) to awaken a literature regional identity in

_____

d) to the region cultural movement throughout the stimulate and unite

_____

24 Look at page 249.

a) What does CDEMA stand for?

_____

b) Broadly speaking, what kind of disasters does CDEMA deal with?

_____

c) More specifically, what four types of disaster does CDEMA deal with?

_____   _____   _____   _____

25 Explain in what ways CARIFESTA might benefit the Caribbean economy.

_____

_____

_____

_____

26 Imagine you are a director of CDEMA responding to the 2010 Haiti earthquake. On a separate sheet, write a paragraph, or a bullet-point list, summing up what kind of immediate action will need to be taken to help the population.

27 Read pages 250–1 of the student book, 'Benefits of regional integration and cooperation'. Explain what is meant by 'free movement of goods, labour and capital' within the Caribbean region.

_____

_____

_____

_____

28 Link these organisations to the things they deal with by drawing lines to link them.

Organisation
CARIFTA
CARICOM/CSME
OECS
ACS
CARIFESTA
CDEMA

What they deal with
Unity
Heritage and sustainable tourism
Culture
Economy
Disaster preparedness
Trade

29 Complete the flowchart below to show how free trade leads to benefits for the Caribbean region. Have a go, then refer to page 251 if you need to.

1 Free trade →

2 Imports are _____ (no tariffs) →

3 More regional _____ are sold

↓

4 More goods are _____

5 More _____ are created ←

6 Increased _____ for workers ←

↓

7 Better _____ of life

30 Read pages 252–3 of the student book, 'Individual role in regional integration'. Say briefly in what three ways individuals can help efforts at regional integration.

_____

_____

_____

31 Tick which of the following you or any of your family have done.

- Taking part in community or regional events such as CARIFESTA
- Helping your neighbours
- Joining a youth group
- Joining a sport club
- Joining a neighbourhood watch group
- Joining any other community group

32 Write a paragraph describing how you or a family member have done any of the things above.

_____

_____

_____

_____

_____

_____

33 Read about CARIFESTA on page 253. From memory or using your imagination, write a present tense account of being at a CARIFESTA event. Try to make the reader feel what it would be like to really be at this event.

_____

_____

_____

_____

_____

_____

_____

_____

_____

_____

1 Read pages 260–1, 'The importance of sustainable use of resources'.

a) What does 'sustainable' mean?

_____

b) Give an example of sustainable tourism.

_____

c) Give an example of unsustainable tourism.

_____

2 Sum up the focus of ecotourism.

_____

3 Read this account by an eco-friendly tourist. Highlight the ways in which she is eco-friendly and write footnotes about each one underneath.

We went to the beautiful Cockpit Country region of Jamaica. I particularly wanted to see the limestone karst environment and study its unique plant life. I was keen to identify plants, so I took photos of those I didn't recognise, rather than picking them to take back to the lodge – which incidentally is run by local people, and supplies food made from locally grown ingredients rather than imported ones.

Our guide was very knowledgeable, and she was very strict about keeping to the trails to avoid damaging the fragile environment – which I was happy to do. We took packed lunches but were very careful to bring any litter back to the lodge. We saw a huge Jamaican boa, which was exciting, but we didn't get too close: we didn't want to disturb it.

_____

_____

_____

_____

_____

_____

4 Identify an area close to where you live, or another location where you could establish an ecotourism lodge. Write a plan for the new facility which will also be offering guided tours. Include:

- its location
- what visitors are likely to see locally
- how you plan to minimise impact on the environment
- where you plan to source water and how it will be used
- how you plan to provide electricity.

5 Research and find out about five eco-tourism attractions or facilities in Jamaica and mark them on the map outline of Jamaica below. Name them and add brief notes about how each one helps to protect local flora and fauna and other resourcs.

Scale 1 : 1 650 000

6 Read pages 262–3 of the student book, 'Sustainability and sustainable practices'.

a) What are the '3 Rs'?

_____

_____

_____

b) What could you do with plastic bags to use them more sustainably?

_____

c) How could you recycle fruit and vegetable peelings?

_____

7 Complete these benefits of the 3 Rs using words from the word bank.

* Less land is needed for _____.
* Natural resources become more _____.
* There are fewer toxic _____ to cause pollution.
* There is less _____ caused by pollution.
* There is less need for _____ disposal services.
* We save _____ by spending less on new goods.

| chemicals | disease | landfill | money | sustainable | waste |

8 Find items around your home that you could recycle into a resource or tool that you could use at school, such as a pencil case. For each item, outline the steps to follow to create the item. Ensure that the steps are detailed so that other students could easily follow them and create similar items of their own.

9 On a separate sheet of paper, write the text for an information leaflet for the National Solid Waste Management Authority (NSWMA). You could write it using questions and answers, like this:

* Who are we? *We are a non-profit-making organisation serving all of Jamaica …*

10 Read pages 264–5 of the student book, 'Responsibility for our environment'. Rearrange these jumbled instructions on how to care for your environment.

Jumbled instruction	Correct instruction
a) always waste a bin for your find	
b) compost kitchen go onto a waste can heap	
c) use water-saving a head shower	
d) when appliances and using lights turn off not them	
e) drop litter not do	
f) turn off your teeth when you water the brush	
g) light energy-efficient bulbs use	

11 Fill in the gaps in this paragraph on eco-friendly travel using the words in the word bank.

Limit your car use and especially your _____ travel. Have your car _____ regularly and _____ at a moderate speed to use less petrol and reduce wear and tear on your car. Use _____ transport or car _____. Even better, ride a _____: it produces no _____ and keeps you fit.

sharing	serviced	public	petrol
emissions	drive	bike	air

12 Answer these questions about ethical consumerism. Use a separate sheet of paper.

a) In your own words, explain who is considered to be an ethical consumer.

b) Visit a local food shop, supermarket or restaurant and make notes on how far these businesses are encouraging customers to practise ethical consumerism or any other sustainable practices. If you have a smartphone, you could take photographs to remind you.

Write a report on your findings to report to your class.

13 Read pages 266–9 of the student book, 'How do production and consumption patterns contribute to sustainability or sustainable development?'.

a) Give one example of a renewable form of energy. _____

b) Give one example of a non-renewable form of energy. _____

c) Explain how we could save trees by using less paper.

_____

d) Where does 'solar' energy come from?

_____

e) What fuel is currently used to produce most of Jamaica's electricity?

_____

f) Explain what 'sustainable' means.

_____

14 Divide the items or activities below into 'Sustainable', 'Non-sustainable' and 'Possibly sustainable' (e.g. paper may be from sustainably grown timber) by writing 'S', 'N' or 'P' next to them.

Air travel for foreign holidays   Wind power

Petrol-based electricity generation   Paper coffee cups in cafés

Plastic coffee cups in cafés   Bamboo-based clothing

Locally grown vegetables   Cycling

Car use   Solar power

15 Answer these questions about tourism in Jamaica.

a) Outline two potential benefits and two potential environmental impacts Jamaica may experience by increasing tourism.

_____

_____

_____

_____

b) On a separate sheet of paper, explain how increased tourism could also prove beneficial for the environment.

16 **Use your notes from the previous activity to write the introduction to a speech arguing for or against the development of tourism in Jamaica. Consider:**

- benefits to the economy
- benefits of conservation to the local environment
- benefits (but also disturbance) to the flora and fauna
- costs of limiting bauxite mining if conservation areas are maintained
- how tourists will travel to and within Jamaica
- the attitude of local people towards tourists.

_____

_____

_____

_____

_____

_____

_____

_____

_____

_____

_____

 17 **Read pages 270–1 of the student book, 'Why we need to protect the environment'.**

a) Biodiversity is:

   i) the university of life

   ii) a dual approach to conservation

   iii) the variety of animals and plants

   iv) an eco-friendly washing power

b) JPAT stands for:

   i) Jamaica Protected Areas Trust

   ii) Junior Person's Attitude Treatment

   iii) Jamaican Public Areas Trust

   iv) Jamaican Parks Authority Team

c) Endemic means:

   i) leading to a conclusion

   ii) relating to a global disease

   iii) rare, threatened

   iv) belonging to a geographical area

18 Underline four factual errors in this paragraph and summarise them below.

The Jamaican government and JPAT bring together conservation groups from the private and public sectors. JPAT strongly promotes the spread of bauxite mining in areas such as the Cockpit Country. It oversees the misuse of conservation funds and supports Jamaica's National Biodiversity Strategy. It also aims to increase tourist hunting of endemic species, particularly those that are endangered. It works to expand public awareness of conservation in protected areas, and to increase public access to these areas by extensive road-building.

_____

_____

_____

_____

19 Write a paragraph explaining why it is important to protect Cockpit Country.

_____

_____

_____

_____

_____

_____

_____

20 Research one of the other protected areas listed on page 271. Write a paragraph to the government arguing that it deserves more funding.

_____

_____

_____

_____

_____

_____

_____

_____

21 Read pages 272–3 of the student book, 'Protected areas of the Caribbean'.

a) In what year did the United Nations set up the SPAW Protocol?

_____

b) Why were the SPAW protocols established in the Caribbean?

_____

22 Select *True* or *False* for these statements.

a) Sea turtles in the Caribbean are in need of protection. *True/False*

b) Hawksbill turtle numbers have increased by 80 per cent over the last ten years. *True/False*

c) Sea turtles' eggs are often taken. *True/False*

d) Shark numbers are falling. *True/False*

e) Sharks fulfil no particular role in marine ecosystems. *True/False*

f) Shark fins are cut off and sold. *True/False*

23 Research the following areas and marine conservation bodies and mark them on the map below. Make notes on what they do and why they are important. Use a separate sheet of paper.

Montego Bay Marine Park

Oracabessa Fish Sanctuary

Discovery Bay Marine Laboratory

Port Royal Marine Laboratory

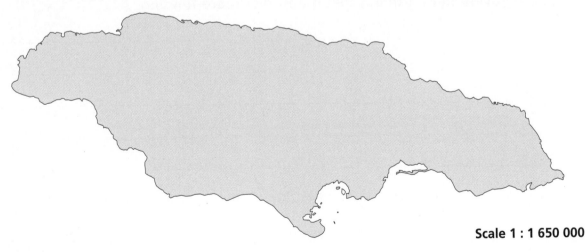

Scale 1 : 1 650 000

Read pages 274–5 of the student book, 'Endangered habitats and species'.

a) What does it mean if a species is 'endangered'?

_____

b) What does it mean if a species becomes 'extinct'?

_____

c) What is meant by 'habitat'?

_____

25 Try this crossword using words in this section.

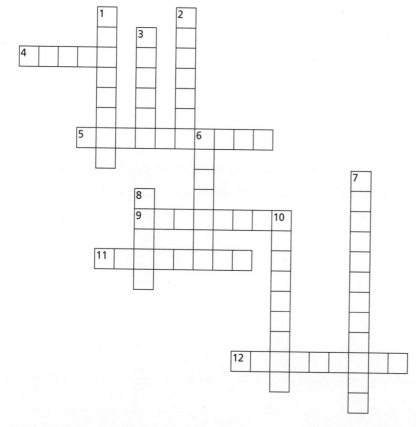

Across	
4.	Animal life
5.	Under threat
9.	Invasive fish threatening other species
11.	Place in danger of extinction
12.	Damaging of habitat, e.g. by chemicals

Down	
1.	Illegal hunting
2.	Removing of forest for timber
3.	Rare Jamaican reptile
6.	When a species has died out
7.	Strategy to save species
8.	Plant life
10.	Endangered turtle

26 Search online for 'invasive alien species Jamaica'. List five invasive plants and five invasive animal species below.

Plants	Animals

27 Research the effects of invasive alien species in Jamaica, and write a report on your findings. Refer to the list above, your research, page 274 (the Jamaican iguana) and the invasive species on page 275. Consider these questions.

- How big a problem are invasive species in Jamaica?
- Why are they a problem? Why should it matter if a new plant such as the African tulip tree begins to spread in Jamaica or elsewhere in the Caribbean?
- Do you think it is better morally to kill off invasive species (e.g. the lionfish) in order to protect native species, or do these invasive species have a right to live?

_____

_____

_____

_____

_____

_____

_____

_____

_____

_____

_____

_____

_____

28 Read pages 276–7 of the student book, 'Conserving our resources'. In your own words, summarise:

a) why we should conserve our resources

_____

_____

_____

b) why Jamaica has set aside areas of land that are given special protection.

_____

_____

_____

29 Explain in your own words:

a) the aims of NEPA

_____

_____

_____

_____

b) why Jamaica's mangroves should be protected.

_____

_____

_____

_____

30 Find out about the benefits of mangroves and how they help to protect against flooding, protect coral reefs and also act as a sanctuary to young marine life.

Use simple materials you can find at home (e.g. a large plastic container or basin, sticks or small branches, water, sand or anything that is available to you) to build a model showing how mangroves are a benefit to us. Add labels to your model so that others can easily interpret what is being illustrated.

31 Read pages 278–9 of the student book, 'Environmental groups in Jamaica'. Explain what you think the following mean:

a) voluntary organisations

_____

b) watchdogs

_____

32 Select *True* or *False* for the following statements.

a) JET stands for Jamaica Environment Trust. *True/False*

b) JET's Schools' Environment Programme began in 1897. *True/False*

c) JET monitors sea turtle nesting. *True/False*

d) NEST is an organisation whose sole aim is to save nesting birds. *True/False*

e) NEST stands for National Environmental Societies Trust. *True/False*

f) NEST's mission is to create environmental problems. *True/False*

g) In the early 1990s, Jamaica was losing forests faster than anywhere else in the world. *True/False*

h) NEST wants to stop ordinary citizens from interfering in environmental conservation. *True/False*

i) NEST works with environmental groups. True/False

33 From your work on environmental issues in Jamaica so far, write a report on Jamaica's progress in environmental conservation. You could include:

- What problems Jamaica has faced (e.g. from mining and logging)
- What government and other organisations are doing to protect the environment
- What ongoing or increasing problems are faced, such as habitat threat and climate change, rising sea levels and pollution.